What's it Like to Live in ...?

Italy

by Jillian Powell

WATERBIRD BOOKS

Columbus, Ohio

Other Titles in This Series:

Canada   France   Jamaica

 Children's Publishing

This edition published in the United State of America in 2003 by
Waterbird Books
an imprint of McGraw-Hill Children's Publishing,
a Division of The McGraw-Hill Companies
8787 Orion Place
Columbus, Ohio 43240-4027

www.MHkids.com

Library of Congress Cataloging-in-Publication Data is on file with the publisher.

© Hodder Wayland 2003

Hodder Wayland is an imprint of Hodder Children's Books

Printed in China.

1-57768-876-7

1 2 3 4 5 6 7 8 9 10 HOD 09 08 07 06 05 04 03

The **McGraw-Hill** Companies

Contents

Where Is Italy?

Italy is in the **Mediterranean region** of southern Europe. It is a long country, shaped like a boot, bordered mostly by the sea.

In Rome, many tourists come to see the Trevi fountain.

◀

Nearly 58 million people live in Italy. Its capital is Rome. Italy is a popular place to visit.

Italy's place in the world

SWITZERLAND

AUSTRIA

SLOVENIA

FRANCE

A l p s

Dolomites

Trieste

Milan

Lake Garda

Venice

Turin

Po

Genoa

Pisa

Arno

Florence

Siena

Tiber

A p e n n i n e s

ITALY

Rome

Pescara

Bari

Brindisi

Naples

ADRIATIC SEA

N

W — E

S

Sardinia

Calgari

Messina

Palermo

Sicily

Siracuse

MEDITERRANEAN SEA

0   100 kilometers

0   100 miles

5

Cities

Many cities in Italy, such as Rome, Florence, and Pisa, started as **settlements** along the banks of a river. Parts of these Italian cities are very old.

The city of Pisa on the Arno River.

Today nearly three million people live in Rome. Most of these people live in the **suburbs** of the city but go into the center to work or shop.

Rome's streets are often full of people.

7

The Landscape

Italy has some high mountains, such as the Alps. It also has large areas of small hills and a wide area of flat **plains**.

The region of Tuscany has a landscape of gentle, rolling hills.

Lake Garda is the largest of the Italian lakes.

Italy has many beautiful lakes.
Its coastline is 4,700 miles long.
Italy's lakes and coastal areas
are popular places to visit.

9

The Weather

Most of Italy has hot, dry summers and mild winters. This is called a Mediterranean climate. The south is hot and dry for most of the year.

Italy is warm and sunny in the summer.

▼

In the winter, skiers enjoy deep snow on the Italian Alps.

In the mountains of the north, summers are short, and the winters are cold and snowy. Spring and fall can be rainy.

Transportation

People travel around Italy in cars, buses, and trains. Motor scooters are a popular means of transportation.

A scooter is a fast way of getting around town.

Ships and boats visit busy ports and harbors, such as Venice, Genoa, and Naples. Rome and Milan have underground trains.

Big cities have cable cars as well as buses.

Farming

Almost a third of Italy is farmland. In the south, farmers grow fruit and vegetables, including grapes and olives.

Italy's sunny climate is ideal for growing grapes.

On the plains, farmers grow grass to use as hay. Others grow grain, such as wheat, for food and use the stalks for **straw**. In the hills, farmers raise sheep and goats.

This farmer is making hay to feed his cattle.

Food

Italians are known for their special foods. Pizza and pasta are favorite Italian foods. There are about 400 different types of pasta!

A chef throws pizza dough into the air to stretch and shape it.

Some regions of Italy are famous for certain foods. Naples is known for its delicious ice cream called *gelato*.

Gelato is a popular treat in Italy, and there are many flavors.

Shopping

Italy has many different kinds of shops. There are large supermarkets and small shops. There are also small outdoor markets that sell bread and cakes or fruit and vegetables.

Italy has colorful, open-air markets.

Big cities have fancy shops that sell designer clothes and other fashion goods.

The Italian designer, Gucci™, is famous for shoes and handbags.

Houses and Homes

In Italian cities, many people live in apartment buildings in the suburbs. Some of the apartments have balconies. There, people sit outside or hang up their laundry to dry.

These homes on the Italian Riviera are apartment buildings.

▼

In the country, more people live in houses than apartments. Many homes are built from stone and have clay tiled roofs.

These country houses are near Lake Garda.

At Work

Italy has many kinds of **industry**, especially in the north. Factories **process** foods and make cars, machinery, chemicals, clothing, and **textiles**.

Italian cars are built in factories and sold all over the world.

Tourism is a very important industry in Italy because it **employs** so many people. There are also many new jobs in **technology**.

Many tourists come to Italy for its climate and to see its beautiful old buildings.

23

Having Fun

Soccer, bicycling, and ball games are popular in Italy. Italians also go to movies or visit **Internet cafés**.

Young people play a game of soccer in the park.

Italians also enjoy watching sports such as **Grand Prix** motorcar racing. Many Italians attend the Giro d'Italia, a bicycle race that tours Italy every spring.

The Italian Grand Prix takes place near Milan every year.

Festivals

In Italy, there are exciting **festivals** and carnivals year-round. Crowds of people come to take part or watch. In February, the biggest festival of the year takes place. It is called Carnival and celebrates the days before Lent begins.

In Venice, people wear colorful masks and costumes for Carnival.

During festivals, there are often races, parades, and **processions** in the streets. Some festivals celebrate religious holidays. Others celebrate seasonal foods such as the mushrooms found in the woods in fall.

The Palio is a famous horse race held in Siena in the summer.

27

Italian Scrapbook

This is a scrapbook of some everyday things you might find in Italy.

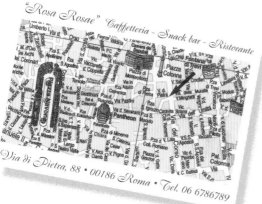

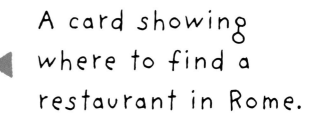

A card showing where to find a restaurant in Rome.

A postcard of the Rialto Bridge in Venice.

Italians make purchases using euros. These can be spent in many countries in Europe.

MUSEO CIVICO DI S. FRANCESCO
MONTEFALCO
ITALIA

Nº 2839

BENOZZO GOZZOLI 1452

A ticket to enter a church museum.

Tickets for taking the bus or train in Italy.

atc
ATC S.p.A. P.I. 00610880379

Il biglietto è valido
soltanto nell'area urbana
di Bologna

Validità 60 minuti

Tariffa BU01
2757886

BIGLIETTO
ORARIO

fermata iniziale

macch.
anno
sett.
giorno
m-p
ore

NG 4969646

Modo di Pagamento
Mode de paiement Cash   WXSDGR

830298280228

02 Posti / Places

Da/De ROMA TERMINI

Partenza / Depart

Compartimento / Compartiment

CORRIDOIO CENTRALE
NON FUMATORI

Riduz. : :
Reduct. : :

TERM. 313 102
P.IVA 05403151003

Valido fino al

CONVALIDARE PRIMA DELLA PARTENZA
Vi abbiamo prenotato/Nous vous avons reserve

PREZZO EUROSTAR
a/a' PERUGIA

Ad.002 Ray

17.50
Numero di posti / Numeros des places

Finestrino/superiore Mediano Corridoio/inferiore
Fenetre/haut   Milieu   Couloir/bas

Cl.
Cl.

2^   006   61   63

L. ****71400
E. ****36,88

Motivo
Motif   NG4969646 BV   0000045

29

Glossary

Employ To give people jobs and provide them with pay.

Euro The money used in some countries in Europe.

Festival A time of celebration.

Grain A crop, such as wheat, grown for food.

Grand Prix A yearly car race.

Industry A business that manufactures a product, such as cars.

Internet café A place where people can meet, use the Internet, and send e-mails.

Mediterranean The areas that border the Mediterranean Sea.

Plain A large area of flat ground.

Process To change something so it is ready for use.

Procession A crowd of people walking as part of a festival or ceremony.

Region A geographical part of a country.

Settlement A place where people have built houses.

Straw Dry cut stalks of grain often used as bedding for animals.

Suburb A living area on the edges of a city.

Technology Work based on computers or machinery.

Textile A woven material used for clothing and the home.

Tourism An industry supported by visitors to a particular country.

Further Information

Some Italian Words

cappuccino	coffee with foamy milk
carnevale	carnival
chiesa	church
gelato	ice cream
grazie	thank you
ferie	feast days/holidays
panetteria	bread shop
per favore	please
piazza	town square
posta	post office
prego	you're welcome
ristorante/trattoria	restaurant

Further Reading From McGraw-Hill Children's Publishing

Giotto and Medieval Art (ISBN 0-87226-315-0)
Leonardo da Vinci (ISBN 0-87226-313-4)
Michelangelo (ISBN 0-87226-319-3)
Picasso (ISBN 0-87226-318-5)
The Sistine Chapel (ISBN 0-87226-638-9)
Women in 19th-Century Europe (ISBN 0-87226-565-X)

Index